Mother of God

Text by Lawrence Cunningham

Photographs by Nicolas Sapieha

Preface by Mary Gordon

Research by Agnese Cini

1817

A Scala Book, Published by Harper & Row, Publishers, San Francisco

Cambridge, Hagerstown, New York, Philadelphia, London, Mexico City, São Paulo, Sidney

Photographs are courtesy Nicolas Sapieha (cover, pp. 1 – 8, 17 – 24, 45, 50 [nos. 3, 6], 51, 57, 77 – 107, 109 – 120); Scala, Florence (pp. 37 – 44, 46 – 47, 50 [nos. 1, 2, 4, 5], 53 – 56, 58 – 60); National Gallery, Washington, D.C. (pp. 48 – 49); Musée Condé, Chantilly, France (p. 52), Durand, Lourdes, France (p. 108).

The Preface by Mary Gordon has been excerpted from her article "Coming to terms with Mary," *Commonweal* CIX:1, 15 January 1982, copyright © 1982 by Mary Gordon; the material is reprinted with the generous permission of Mary Gordon and *Commonweal*.

Designed by Armando Milani
Produced by Scala, Florence, Italy
Project directed by Maria Teresa Train
Printed in Italy by Amilcare Pizzi s.p.a.

FIRST EDITION

Library of Congress Cataloging in Publication Data

Cunningham, Lawrence.
  Mother of God.

  "A Scala book."
  1. Mary, Blessed Virgin, Saint.   I. Sapieha, Nicholas.
II. Title.
BT602.C86   1982   232.91   82-47741
ISBN 0-06-061653-9

82 83 84 85 86 10 9 8 7 6 5 4 3 2 1

Contents

Preface

Mary Gordon

I have wanted to create for myself a devotion to Mary that honors her as woman, as mother. I wanted this particularly as I grew older; I longed for it with a special poignance as I experienced motherhood for the first time. One must find isolated words, isolated images; one must travel the road of metaphor, of icon, to come back to that figure who has moved the hearts of men and women and abides shining, worthy of our love, compelling it.

I have chosen three qualities in my thoughts about her: innocence, grief, and glory. I offer here no system, but a set of meditations. I offer no final words, since, for a woman to come to terms with this woman who endures beloved despite a history of hatred, she must move lightly and discard freely; she must take upon herself the ancient labor of women: she must become a gatherer, a hoarder. She must put out for those around her scattered treasure, isolates without a pattern whose accumulated meaning comes from the relations of proximity.

Innocence, grief, glory: they are potent words, ideas, and like all human things that take on power are susceptible to perversion and corruption. The beautiful idea of innocence can be perverted, in the face of a generalized hostility to female power, to an ideal of subservience, of a loss of individual identity and autonomy, of an enforced childishness which barters the responsibilities of freedom for the privileges of a protected object. But the ideal of innocence has nothing to do with weakness. On the contrary, real innocence is capable of understanding and confronting evil in its most radical terms: it is undeceived about the Powers of Darkness, and does not confuse them with human frailty; it never forgets compassion.

Innocence: it is a rare and a powerful quality; it is not the failure of the imagination to imagine wrong, but the naturally bestowed inability to choose malice, selfishness. It is the inborn lack of that instinct to touch others for their harm; the absence of the desire to inflict pain. Mary embodies our love for this instinctive purity of life. I imagine her in one of Leonardo's Annunciations covered over with light, sure in her youthful self-knowledge. Humble—"Behold the handmaid of the Lord"—yet never cringing, always aware of the great dignity of her position: "All generations shall call me blessed." Her consent asked for by God, not enforced. Innocence suggests an inviolable goodness, not striven for, but lavishly and freely given. Hence we value it. It is not the virtue some of us struggle a lifetime to attain. It is a kind of luck. Grace, we call it. The love of innocence is the celebration of grace.

I call up more images. A sixteenth century sculpture I saw in Winchester Cathedral. Mary the young girl looks amused. Her mouth, a thin indentured curve, turns up with pleasure. Her downcast eyes show what might be fear, but finally is not, but only an inward looking, an understanding, wary, perhaps, but not overwhelmed. I think of the curve of the body of a thirteenth century statue of the young Mother with her child. At ease in its own nature, swaying almost with the rhythms of maternal love, ready for life, radically open to experience, to love.

This radical openness is what Karl Rahner sees as the importance of the idea of virginity for Christians regardless of their sexual vocation. "This attitude of expectation, of readiness and receptivity to grace, this awareness that the ultimate thing is grace and grace alone, is something which, as an attitude of mind every Christian must have, even if it does not find concrete expression in virginity."

I think of the young woman in Fra Angelico's Annunciation; thunderstruck from the force of the Angel's entrance, serene, and pleased. I remember the face of the young Mary in Pasolini's *Gospel According to St. Matthew.* A sensual girl, her wide mouth turned up in a smile of comprehending expectation. A girl of the Middle East, of the warm air of a temperate climate, picking fruit, walking on warm nights under stars we can no longer in the modern world imagine.

Yet these images have nothing to do with the false images of innocence used in our culture to sell everything from designer jeans to membership in the Moral Majority. Contrast the image of the girl in Pasolini's movie, of Fra Angelico's virgin, of the thirteenth century young mother, the sensual curve of her hip ready for motion—contrast these images with the image of a young woman in Jerry Falwell's school. The sureness of the young Mary is a sureness born of grace; it is a sureness that never excludes understanding of human suffering, that does not assert with every flick of its coiffed head the exclusive rightness of its position. It is an innocence that is rooted in the love of the physical world. It is an innocence saddened by much, surprised at nothing. It is an innocence that knows it will be pierced by a sword, ground under by great scandal of an unjust world. It is an innocence that lives with the knowledge of its own impending grief.

The grieving mother. *Mater Dolorosa.* The second word I think about is grief. I note that in our culture, fixated as it is on youth, there are far fewer images of the sorrowing mother, who would have to be at least middle-aged, than of the young virgin with child. I listen to Pergolesi's *Stabat Mater.* A mature grief, grief rescued from the danger of madness, not Clytemnestra raging, vengeful over her lost child, but a mother silenced by sorrow. Only in the heart, the great music of a resignation that is anything but a flat giving in: a lifting of the heart to God in the face of the absurd. The death of one's child. It is, for many of us, the worst we can imagine, the greatest stumbling block to faith. To witness the ignominious death of one's most innocent child! In Mary we have the emblem of all human sorrow, innocence victimized by injustice, by the incomprehensible exigencies of the cruel God who is the God of love. I see her overcome with grief, swooning from the violence of the blows of God, her Father and her Son, in Grünewald's rendering of the Sorrowing Mother. For this woman, there is no comfort. The heart pierced with the sword, now open to the world. The sweet compassion of the innocent girl deepened beyond our comprehension. Spared nothing. We bring to her the scandal of the fallen world; we give our despair, the failure of all human consolation to assuage us.

I see Bellini's Pietá. The Virgin is bent over the dead body of her Son. But behind her, the winter landscape blossoms with the first flowers of spring. She is the mother of the Resurrected Christ; that too is in her fate as she lies holding her dead child. We can, in a romantic love of suffering, fixate on the Sorrowing Virgin, perverting even that image in the belief that we are facing the true nature of life. But for a Christian, the final nature of life is triumphant. Christ rises from the dead: his mother takes her place beside him at the Throne of God.

Triumph. How easily that too can be perverted to the triumphalism that attaches to the Queenship of Mary when the church sees itself politically beleaguered, in danger of losing its power on earth. Marina Warner notes: "In times of stasis and entrenchment, as under Popes Pius XII and to some extent Paul VI, veneration of the Virgin is encouraged, and in times of strong ecumenism and change, when the church is less self-righteous and assured, devotion to the Virgin, especially under her triumphant aspect, is restrained and declines." What can we make of this? The image of the woman brought out as a weapon to threaten the rebellious? Yes, of course, if we confuse the Queenship of Mary with a human rule whose first goal is to keep everyone in line. But how ridiculous. The triumph of Mary is beyond law, and lawlessness; the notion of disobedience is a paltry irrelevance if one imagines choirs of angels and the mother of God enthroned, not above her children, but in the midst of them, their voices raised in a harmony impossible to them in their life on earth. I see gold and ivory; I imagine the music of Handel, Alexander's Feast. The Mother of God is the Queen of Heaven; she presides over a feast, secure that all her children are, at last, well fed.

In the end, it is beyond reason, beyond argument. In the end, the devotion to Mary is the objective correlative of all the primitive desires that lead human beings to the life of faith. She embodies our desire to be fully human yet to transcend death. The hatred of women is the legacy of death; in Mary, Mother and Queen, we see, enfleshed in a human form that touches our most ancient longings, the promise of salvation, of deliverance, through flesh, from the burdens of flesh. As Hopkins says:

> If I have understood,
> She holds high motherhood
> Toward all our ghostly good
> And plays in grace her part
> About man's beating heart,
> Laying, like air's fine flood,
> The deathdance in his blood.

I think, finally, it is through poetry, through painting, sculpture, music, through those human works that are magnificently innocent of the terrible strain of sexual hatred by virtue of the labor, craft, and genius of their great creators, that one finds the surest way back to the Mother of God.

Magnificat

My soul magnifies the Lord,
and my spirit rejoices in God my Savior;
because he has regarded the lowliness
   of his handmaid;
for, behold, henceforth all generations
   shall call me blessed;
because he who is mighty has done
   great things for me,
and holy is his name.
His mercy is from generation to generation
   on those who fear him.
He has shown might with his arm,
he has scattered the proud in the conceit
   of their heart.
He has put down the mighty from their thrones,
   and has exalted the lowly.
He has filled the hungry with good things,
   and the rich he has sent away empty.
He has given help to Israel, his servant,
   mindful of his mercy,
even as he spoke to our fathers,
   to Abraham and to his posterity forever.

Ave Maria

Ave Maria, gratia plena, Dominus tecum.
Benedicta tu in mulieribus
et benedictus fructus ventris tui, Jesus.
Sancta Maria, mater Dei,
ora pro nobis peccatoribus
nunc et in hora mortis nostrae.
Amen.

Mary in the Bible

The New Testament portrait of Mary is, like everything in the biblical text, artlessly simple, tantalizingly enigmatic, and religiously inexhaustible. Were one to follow the narrative of her life in the New Testament by "harmonizing" the various accounts in the Gospels of Luke and Matthew (which provide the fullest pictures of her early life) with the incidents recorded in the Gospel of John (which gives us the most complete vignettes of her life while Jesus was engaged in his active ministry), the story would reflect those familiar scenes that most of us have seen in the great religious art of the Western world.

The story begins abruptly with the vision of an angel, a constant sign in the Bible that something momentous is to happen. The angel Gabriel appears to a young woman named Mary and, after saluting her as one "highly favored" (Luke 1:28),* tells her that she is to bear a son who will be named Jesus. This child will "be great and will be called Son of the Most High. He will rule over the House of Jacob for ever and his reign will have no end" (Luke 1:33). Mary responds to this announcement with puzzlement ("But how can this come about, since I am a virgin?" Luke 1:34). The angel answers that her conception will be the work of the Holy Spirit and adds, as if to demonstrate the truth of his assertion, that her cousin Elizabeth has conceived a son in her old age. Mary responds with alacrity to the announcement: "I am the handmaid of the Lord. Let what you have said be done to me" (Luke 1:38).

After this annunciation scene, Mary hastens to the hill country of Judea to visit her pregnant cousin who, on Mary's arrival, salutes her with words that are now part of one of Christendom's most common prayers: "Blessed art though amongst women and blessed is the fruit of thy womb!" Elizabeth

---

* All quotations are taken from the *Jerusalem Bible* unless otherwise noted.

says that the child of her own womb—the future John the Baptizer—"leapt with joy" at Mary's arrival. Mary, in turn, responds with a canticle that has become one of the favorite prayers of the Christian church. Called the "Magnificat" (from its opening word in the Latin version of the prayer), it is suffused with the messianic piety of the Hebrew scriptures:

> My soul proclaims the greatness of the Lord
> and my spirit exults in God my saviour;
> because he has looked upon his lowly handmaid.
> Yes, from this day forward all generations will call me blessed,
> for the Almighty has done great things for me.
> Holy is his name,
> and his mercy reaches from age to age for those who fear him.
> He has shown the power of his arm,
> he has routed the proud of heart.
> He has pulled down princes from their thrones and exalted the lowly.
> The hungry he has filled with good things, the rich sent away empty.
> He has come to the help of Israel his servant, mindful of his mercy
> —according to the promise he made to our ancestors—
> of his mercy to Abraham and to his descendants forever.
>
> (Luke 1:46—55)

Mary's intended husband Joseph, learning of her pregnancy, wished to put her away to avoid a public scandal, but is told by an angel in a dream that he should take Mary to wife, since "she has conceived what is in her by the Holy Spirit" (Matt. 1:20).

Joseph and Mary leave their home in Nazareth to go to Bethlehem to register for a Roman census. Jesus is born in Bethlehem, presumably in a stable, since Luke notes that the newborn infant was laid in a manger (a food trough for animals) as "there was no room for them in the inn" (Luke 2:7). Shepherds in the nearby fields hear of the child's birth from an angel who announces "news of great joy" about a "saviour who has been born to you, who is Christ the Lord." The scene, familiar to all who know the Christmas story, ends with an angelic host singing a hymn of praise. As the shepherds make their obeisance to the newborn infant, the gospel says that, "as for Mary, she treasured all these things and pondered them in her heart" (Luke 2:19). This allusive phrase has never been fully explained, but it most likely means that Mary was the link between these early events and the later ministry of Jesus.

Luke then goes on to say that Jesus was circumcised according to the demands of the Law and that Mary later went up to the temple for her own rites of purification after the birth of the child. In this temple scene, two ancient prophetic figures—Simeon and Anna—praise the child. The praise of Simeon has become the common night prayer of monks and nuns over the centuries. It is called "Nunc Dimittis," after its first words in Latin:

Now, master, you can let your servant go in peace,
just as you promised;
because my eyes have seen the salvation
which you have prepared for all the nations to see,
a light to enlighten the pagans
and the glory of your people Israel.

(Luke 2:29 – 32)

Simeon's prophetic praise for the infant Jesus finished, he turns his gaze on the Virgin and speaks directly to her: "You see this child: he is destined for the fall and the rising of many in Israel, destined to be a sign that is rejected—and a sword will pierce your own soul too—so that the secret thoughts of many may be laid bare" (Luke 2:34 – 35). What this "sword" is has been the subject of much speculation throughout the centuries. Did the sword refer to her own moments of doubt or to her putative martyrdom as some of the early Fathers thought? Or does this scene presage the sorrowful mother at the foot of the cross as Catholic piety has believed? Does it represent the word of God as Saint Ambrose has suggested? Or the future fall of Jerusalem? The "sword" is one of those many references about which unanimity has not been achieved.

According to Matthew's gospel, wise men from the East "had seen his star" and had come to Bethlehem to pay homage to the child, offering him gifts of "gold, frankincense, and myrrh." The presence of these exotic figures aroused the suspicions of King Herod, who was determined to track down the child whom the wise men honored. To neutralize any rivals for his power, Herod adopted the gruesome expediency of slaughtering all male infants in the area. In a poignant passage, the evangelist sees this as a fulfillment of Jeremiah's words about Rachel "weeping for her children, refusing to be comforted because they were no more." Having been warned in a dream to avoid this slaughter, Mary and Joseph flee to Egypt with the child and remain there until an angel tells Joseph of Herod's death. They then return to settle in the town of Nazareth.*

Of the childhood of Jesus we know practically nothing. Luke tells us that when he was twelve, he went with Joseph and Mary to Jerusalem for the Passover feast. Jesus was separated from his parents, who subsequently found him teaching in the temple, seated among the doctors of the Law. When his mother remonstrated him about his absence, Jesus responded that he had to be about his Father's business. The scene then concludes with this brief, and final, statement about the youth of Jesus:

> He then went down with them and came to Nazareth and lived under their authority. His mother stored up all these things in her heart. And Jesus increased in wisdom, in stature, and favor with God and men. (Luke 2:51 — 52)

With that anecdote, the accounts of the childhood of Jesus close. Of his hidden years at Nazareth the Gospels tell us nothing. The imaginings of the later apocryphal tales are of no help, since they tend to portray Jesus as a little tyrant who could use his hidden powers to create fantastic toys or punish those who would defy him in any way. When his public ministry begins, we presume Jesus to be about thirty years of age. Joseph has receded into the background (and perhaps has died by this time), and Mary is mentioned only a few times in the synoptic gospels and not always in a seemingly flattering light. In Mark's gospel, for instance, she appears in only one scene (3:31 — 35) and there she seems to be repudiated by Jesus. Mary merits but one other mention in Mark's gospel, when people in his hometown of Nazareth marvel at his audacity at preaching and say: "This is the carpenter, surely, the son of Mary . . ." (Mark 6:3; cf. parallel passages where this verse is modified to underscore other emphases — Matt. 13:55, Luke 4:22, and John 6:42). After the infancy accounts, neither Luke nor Matthew treats Mary in any extended way. Saint Paul, the earliest of the New Testament writers, never mentions Mary by name and makes only one specific reference to Jesus as being "born of a woman" (Gal. 4:4)

Saint John's gospel, in contrast to the synoptics, sets out two important vignettes in which Mary plays a central role. These scenes are set like markers

---

* How this account of the flight can be reconciled with Luke's account is a difficult, if not insoluble, problem. On the infancy accounts, see Raymond E. Brown's magisterial study, *The Birth of the Messiah* (Garden City, N.Y.: Doubleday, 1977), in which the problems are set out and proposals for a reading of the infancy texts are proposed.

at the beginning of the public career of Jesus and at its culmination on Calvary.

At a wedding feast in the town of Cana, Mary and her son are in attendance. Mary notices a shortage of wine and brings that fact to the attention of Jesus. Jesus, in turn, changes water into wine, to the general amazement of the crowd. John ends his narration of this miracle with these words: "This was the first sign given by Jesus; it was given at Cana in Galilee. After this he went down to Capernaum with his mother and brothers but they stayed there only a few days" (John 2:11–12).

John's other reference to Mary (who, incidentally, is never called by name—Jesus refers to her simply as "Woman") appears in his account of the crucifixion of Jesus. The scene is so famous that it deserves to be told in the words of the evangelist. Jesus has already been raised up on his cross. John, alone of the evangelists, notes the presence of Mary at the crucifixion:

> Near the cross of Jesus stood his mother and his mother's sister, Mary the wife of Clopas, and Mary of Magdala. Seeing his mother and the disciple he loved standing near her Jesus said to his mother, "Woman, this is your son." Then to the disciple he said, "This is your mother." And from that moment the disciple made a place for her in his home. (John 19:25–27)

In Acts 1:14, Mary is described as being part of the small Jerusalem community along with the apostles, the women, and the brothers of Jesus. Beyond that, nothing. The New Testament does not tell us how long she lived, with whom, or where; neither are we given any information about her death or her relation to the nascent Christian community. The silence about Mary's later life parallels the gospel's silence about her origins. The gospel abruptly introduces us to a woman of child-bearing age but tells us nothing about her immediate antecedents, her family, social status, or her daily life. We know of Mary only in relationship to the story of Jesus the Christ, a fact that is theologically significant and not always recognized.

It was inevitable that the Christian imagination would supply what the New Testament failed to provide. Beginning in the middle of the second century and continuing for some centuries thereafter, apocryphal accounts of those hidden times, often attributed to apostolic sources, began to appear in Christian circles.

The *Protoevangelium of James* (circa A.D. 150/180) is the earliest Christian book that shows an independent interest in the life of Mary. Attributed to the apostle James (the "brother of the Lord," as he is described in the New Testament), this work names Mary's parents as Anna and Joachim, insists that she served God in the Jerusalem temple as a devoted virgin, depicts Joseph as an elderly widower with children from a first marriage who is betrothed to Mary through divine intervention, states that Jesus was born in a cave, and fleshes out other marian themes. This book, ancient as it is, does not represent a genuine historical memory about Mary nor was it ever accepted as part of the authoritative canon of inspired writings by the Christian church. Nonetheless, the *Protoevangelium of James* had a certain prestige within circles of popular piety and provided a fertile ground for the Christian imagination. It had certain obvious things to recommend it. Its depiction of Saint Joseph as an elderly widower made Mary's virginity more secure in the minds of many and provided a handy way of explaining that the "brothers and sisters of the Lord" were children from Joseph's first marriage. The many "lives of the Virgin" in art, culminating in the great fresco cycle done by Giotto in Padua for the Arena Chapel, owe their inspiration to this ancient piece of marian hagiography.

Later apocryphal works filled in, often with elaborately fanciful detail, stories about the life of the Virgin, events during the flight into Egypt, anecdotes about the "hidden years" at Nazareth, and so on. There were also stories about the Virgin's last days, including one tale that describes how she went to Ephesus (where a house of the Virgin is still venerated) with Saint John and miraculously reappeared in Jerusalem where she "fell asleep" in the presence of the apostles. Saint Thomas alone did not witness this miracle because, true to his doubting nature, he came late only to see a tomb that now was empty since the Virgin had been assumed into heaven. These stories were told and retold, supplemented by later medieval "revelations." Their influence is apparent in art and popular piety throughout history to the present day.

All of these stories, both the early and late ones, reflect a common impulse in the hagiographical tradition to extend, embroider, and amplify for reasons of edification or theological explanation. Their importance rests in the insights they give us into the mentality of early Christianity as it tried to fill in the gaps in the gospel stories or to make theological points with new stories.

The marian elaborations of the early church also underscore a basic fact about the New Testament accounts of Mary: they are not the simple, naive narratives that they appear to be at first reading. They are not examples of pious folklore. Centuries of study, reflection, and commentary on the relatively few verses that mention Mary have helped us to understand their complexity and theological depth. Modern scholarship, in fact, has come to a startling conclusion about the marian passages: they are not biographical fragments, but highly allusive and tautly rendered statements of theological belief reflecting the concerns and faith of the early Christian community. Such conclusions from marian scholarship help to explode the oft-repeated charge that mariological beliefs are late accretions to Christianity. It is true that there has been a development in our understanding of Mary, but, in fact, as critical scholarship has shown, the marian passages reflect a deep theological understanding about Mary, who in the New Testament writings has taken on an exemplary and symbolical role in explaining the early church's faith in Jesus the Christ.

Since this text accompanies some famous examples of marian painting, perhaps an analogy from art will help make this point more dramatically. At first glance, Fra Angelico's Annunciation (pp. 40 – 41) is simplicity itself. It seems to tell a very direct story with extreme economy. The angel Gabriel appears at the left of the painting, announcing his momentous news to the placidly composed figure of Mary at the right of the scene. The whole story is framed in an open architectural setting with a garden off to one side. On closer examination, however, this simple fresco shows itself to be dense with symbolism and polyvalent meanings. The colors of the angel's wings, the gold of the halo, and the blue of the Virgin's mantle all have their specific theological significance. The enclosed garden to the left of the scene (the traditional *hortus conclusus* of medieval art) symbolizes the virginity of Mary. The flowers in that garden, rendered faithfully from Fra Angelico's observations of the Tuscan countryside, have their symbolic significance. The austerely bare room in which Mary sits recalls Saint Augustine's observation that the sinless "sweep clean the room of their souls." The window behind the virgin may well be the common medieval symbol of Mary's virginity in the birth process itself, suggesting that Jesus passed through the body of Mary just as light passes through glass. At the base of the fresco (it is in the Dominican convent of San Marco in Florence) is this admonition to the friars: "Venerating this figure of the Virgin as you pass by, do not fail to say an 'Ave Maria.'"

What therefore appears, at first glance, to be a simple narrative painting of the Annunciation, is, in fact, a complex work that makes many allusions to the virtues of the Virgin by using theological, devotional, and hortatory material. The fresco was designed not to tell a story, but to remind the friars to enlarge their sense of devotion and piety. The painter's intention was to instruct as well as to inform. The density of the painting's meaning only becomes clear when the viewer understands where the painting is situated and knows something about the symbolic language of fifteenth-century Christian piety.

If we turn from Fra Angelico's painting of the Annunciation to the account of the Annunciation (Luke 1:26 – 38) on which it is based, we see in those thirteen terse verses the same kind of complexity. We also see some significant differences. Fra Angelico had to visualize his scene without the aid of any descriptive hints from the evangelist. Luke does not tell us in his narrative the time of day the angel appeared, what the angel looked like, how Mary was dressed, where the actual Annunciation took place in Nazareth, how old Mary was, and what she was doing when the angel appeared to her. The message, not the setting, concerned the evangelist. And it is important to note that fact because almost every painting in this work interprets the literary text to the extent that it supplies what is missing. In that sense, marian paintings are commentaries on marian biblical passages.

At first glance, the biblical account of the Annunciation is as simple and unadorned as the fresco of Fra Angelico: the angel appears to a startled young woman, reassures her, and tells her that she will be the mother of an extraordinary child. The woman is puzzled since she is a virgin, but the angel insists that her child will be born through the power of God. Mary accepts the announcement and the "angel goes away, leaving her" (Luke 1:38).

Only when we begin to look more closely at this narrative and its dialogue do we begin to see both its richness and its structural complexity. The narrative itself parallels the description of another announcement that appears in an earlier part of this same chapter: the angel's visit to Zechariah, which foretold the birth of John the Baptizer. Luke, the careful writer, thus provides some literary symmetry to the intertwined narratives of the infancy of John and Jesus in his first two chapters.

It is not only a question of structures that seem crafted and nuanced. The angel greets Mary as one who is "highly favored" (Greek: *kecharitomene*).

That phrase, when rendered into Hebrew, produces the name Hannah, and Hannah was the mother of the prophet Samuel. Allusions to Hannah also occur later in Luke's narrative—in Mary's hymn, the "Magnificat." Again, the angel tells Mary that her son will be born, despite her virginity, because the "Holy Spirit will come upon you, and the power of the Most High will cover you with its shadow" (Luke 1:35). In that line are echoes of the prophet Isaiah promising the future advent of the Davidic Messiah on whom the "spirit of Yahweh rests" (Isa. 11:2). The act of the Holy Spirit "overshadowing" Mary reminds us instinctively of the divine presence on the mount of Transfiguration overshadowing the glorified Jesus (cf. Luke 9:34). Some scholars have also argued that the same phrase alludes to the mysterious presence of God in the Old Testament ark of the covenant so that, in Luke's portrait, Mary was the new ark of the covenant.

To view art intelligently, one must develop an eye; to read scripture properly, one must develop an ear. We do not only read scriptures with the eye, we listen to them. Listening to the marian texts brings us echoes of the prophets and the mothers of the prophets, the faith of the early church, as well as the literary sensitivity of the writer Luke who told his readers that before he wrote his gospel, he carefully went over "the whole story from the beginning" (Luke 1:3).

Luke is usually regarded, along with John, as the most refined and literary of the New Testament writers. His words form a rich composite picture. It may be that this skill triggered the legend that Saint Luke was also a painter. He is the patron saint of painters in the Roman Catholic church and more than one ancient painting has been attributed to him. On the Greek orthodox peninsula of Mount Athos, at least three icons are exhibited as having come from the palette of the saint. Flemish painters of the fifteenth century often depicted Luke as painting portraits of the Virgin. While these stories belong to the tradition of pious folklore, they reveal a sensible instinct: that Luke was, in his own way, an artist with a profound and rich vision.

A close study of art can thus aid us to read the New Testament with an equal sense of nuance. We can "see" the stories of the Bible at first reading, but only when we understand the circumstances under which these stories were written, and their purpose, do we begin to get some idea of their complexity and how we are to respond to them. What, for example, are we to make of Mary's "Magnificat," which is part of the visitation story? Does its insistent contrast of the rich and powerful with the poor and lowly reflect a deeper link with Luke's overall interest in the downtrodden, the poor, the weak, the outcast Samaritans, and the other unfortunates who people his account of Jesus? What is the relationship of this canticle to Luke's version of the Sermon on the Mount? Is Mary to be seen in this passage, as many scholars think, as representative of the "Poor Ones" (Hebrew: *anawim*) who yearned for the redemption of Israel and who figure so prominently in many of the Hebrew psalms? What significance are we to give to the fact that "Magnificat" parallels very closely the canticle sung by Hannah, the mother of the prophet Samuel, in the Old Testament (cf. 1 Sam. 2:1–10)? What point is Luke trying to make? Does this whole scene reflect the faith of early Jewish Christians who were deeply indebted to the concept of the "Poor Ones of Israel"? Such issues begin to be raised only when these "simple" stories are given a deeper study.

Other marian passages that strike us, at first reading, as enigmatic or harsh take on a new depth when studied in this holistic way. In Saint John's gospel, for example, Jesus habitually addresses his mother as "Woman." Her name is never mentioned by the evangelist. Scholars assure us that there is no evidence that such a form of address was a usual one, either in Hebrew or in Greek, for a son to use with his mother. To our ears, in fact, it sounds peremptory and cold. What are we to make of this strange form of address, so peculiar to John's gospel? Many commentators think that the term *woman* was used by the fourth evangelist to invoke the memory of Eve, the first woman. The Eve/Mary parallel was already suggested by the Christian writer Justin Martyr in the second century. Was this also John's intention in his gospel? We do know that the prologue of his work has a conscious echo of the opening lines of the Book of Genesis so that his gospel shows awareness of being a book of the new creation. If John was attempting to invoke the figure of Eve, then it is apparent that he has already given a theological (as opposed to a merely historical) interpretation of Mary in his gospel. If Mary is a new symbolical Eve, then two other famous texts that are often applied to her may have to be viewed against this background: the woman in Genesis 3:15 whose offspring will be at enmity with the offspring of the serpent tempter and the woman, "adorned with the sun, standing on the moon" in Revelation 12:1, who is often seen in the Christian tradition as a complex representation of Israel, the church, and Mary, the mother of Christ.

Whole libraries have been written on these and other passages that deal with the person of Mary. The historical and technical issues are too complex and too debated to consider here. Our purpose is only to hint at the depth of these issues, to encourage the interested person to take another look, and to realize that, even in taking a second look, only the surface has been skimmed. We must understand that the great art, sculpture, architecture, poetry, music, devotional literature, theology, and religious movements that have sprung from the marian tradition are rooted, finally, in simple narratives that are, at the same time, richly complex theological constructs. The complexity of these narratives derives, as we have noted, from the dense biblical tradition that undergirds them. Beyond that, however, these simple stories also have the power to invoke ceaseless meditation and constant reinterpretation because, in their simplicity, they hint at issues that touch the very fabric of human existence and human longing. When all is said by the theologians and exegetes, the marian stories of the New Testament speak on the human level of the great mysteries of human sexuality, birth, and motherhood, as well as the religious mysteries of divine intentions, the human reality of belief, the hope of redemption, and its actualization in the common currency of life. That is why readers can go back to the narratives again and again. And that is why artists could ever return to the theme though it had been done many times before.

For Further Reading

The literature on Mary in the Bible is immense, of varying quality, and often incredibly technical. The following books have been most helpful to me: J. McHugh, *The Mother of Jesus in the New Testament* (Garden City, N.Y.: Doubleday, 1975); R. E. Brown et al., eds., *Mary in the New Testament* (Philadelphia: Fortress, 1978); R. E. Brown, *The Birth of the Messiah: A Commentary on the Infancy Narratives in Matthew and Luke* (Garden City, N.Y.: Doubleday, 1977). These three books have excellent bibliographies for further study, and they reflect the most recent scholarship from an ecumenical perspective. For a more mainline Catholic reading of the marian texts, I have been aided by Pierre Grelot, "Marie (Saint Vierge)," in *Dictionnaire de Spiritualité* (Paris: Beauchesne, 1977), col. 409 – 423. For the development of marian themes in the postbiblical period, the standard work is Hilda Graef, *Mary: A History of*

Doctrine and Devotion, 2 vols. (New York: Sheed and Ward, 1963). For a recent synthetic attempt to assess the New Testament picture of Mary, I have found helpful the suggestive article of Patrick Bearsley, "Mary the Perfect Disciple," *Theological Studies* (September, 1980), pp. 461 – 504.

44

54

Mary in the Western Christian Tradition

Nearly a generation ago, the Lutheran theologian Wolfhart Pannenberg noted that christology is the explication of the significance of an historical event while mariology attempts to personify characteristic responses in faith to that event. Mary, concluded Pannenberg, is far more important in the history of Christianity as a symbol than as an historical person. There is much truth in what Pannenberg writes. What he notes about theology is all the more significant when consideration is given to the place of Mary in the long development of Western religious culture in general. In fact, as Henry Adams argued at the turn of the century, the Virgin was every bit as essential for a symbolic understanding of the Middle Ages as the dynamo was for understanding his own age. "He was only too glad," Adams wrote in *The Education of Henry Adams* of his first encounter with Gothic cathedrals, "to yield himself entirely, not to her charm or to any sentimentality of religion, but to her mental and physical energy of creation which had built up these World's Fairs of thirteenth century force that turned Saint Louis and Chicago pale."

To track the role of Mary in the religious imagination of Christianity is to get a compressed tour, not only of theological development, but of the metaphorical and symbolic yearnings of the various Christian ages of the past. It is both fascinating and instructive—if not downright paradoxical—to consider that biblical religion, so unremittingly masculine in its emphasis on Yahweh and his Son, should hold up for our veneration a figure who was to enshrine what was perceived by Christianity to be the essence of femininity.

Mary as feminine, of course, was proposed under a number of rubrics: the woman who was virgin, spouse, handmaid, mother, queen, helper, mediatrix, and fulfillment of the Old Testament prophecies. Those titles, however, have always stood in some sort of tension. Mary is the virgin who is a mother; the handmaid who is a queen; the simple representative of the poor of Israel who is the "woman clothed with the sun." The tensions become more pronounced when one accepts that Mary bore divinity within her. The scriptures never fully explored that paradox, but the Christian imagination certainly did. The lovely, naive *Nativity Play* from medieval York has Mary address her newborn child in this fashion:

> Hail, my Lord God! Hail, Prince of Peace!
> Hail, my Father and hail my son!
> Hail, sovereign warrior who routs all sin!
> Hail, God and man on earth to dwell!
> . . . Son, as I am the simple subject of thine,
> Vouchsafe me, sweet son, I pray thee,
> That I might take thee in these arms of mine
> And in this poor garment wrap thee.
> Grant me this bliss since
> I am thy mother chosen to be in steadfastness.*

One senses in this simple (and anachronistic) scene the startling paradox of a mother praying to her newborn infant. The implications of that paradox were made in an even more striking manner by John Donne in the sestet of his justly famous sonnet, "The Annunciation":

> Ere, by the spheres time was created, thou
> Wast in his mind—which is thy son and brother,
> Whom thou conceivest—conceived; and the Father's Mother:
> Thou hast Light in dark, and shut in little room
> Immensity, cloistered in thy dear womb.

Such tensions and paradoxes are found throughout the history of Christianity; they are graphically illustrated by two views of the Virgin in the period of the church Fathers. In the third and fourth centuries, there was a great surge of interest in asceticism in Christian circles. As the Roman Empire in the West seemed more and more to be in its final agony, thousands of men and women fled to the deserts to live incredibly harsh lives of penance and solitude. To these "athletes of Christ," the person of Mary the Virgin was set

---

* I have modernized the English.

forth as a paradigmatic figure. Mary was praised as a model of humility, retirement, obedience, and chastity. An anonymous Coptic treatise of the fourth century, for example, depicted Mary living a life of continuous prayer and fasting, being watched over and ministered to by angels, and totally separated from the larger world around her. St. Jerome's fierce defense of Mary's virginity was rooted in his bias towards the ascetic life. The early apocryphal writings that depicted Mary as living in hidden holiness as a servant in the temple (before her engagement to Joseph) presented a powerful image for the hidden life of the solitary servant of God. This "hiddenness" of Mary and her penitential stance is touchingly illustrated in this remembrance taken from the early desert Fathers:

> Abba Joseph related that Abba Isaac said, "I was sitting with Abba Poemen one day and I saw him in ecstasy and, as I was on great terms of freedom of speech with him, I prostrated myself before him and begged him saying, 'Tell me where you were.' He was forced to answer and he said, 'My thought was with Mary, the Mother of God, as she wept by the cross of the saviour. I wish I could always weep like that.'"*

Mary as the hidden ascetic stood in contrast to that Mary proposed for veneration by those Christians who exalted her person because of her maternal connection with the Incarnation. The same centuries that saw the rise of asceticism also saw fierce theological wars concerning questions of the Trinity and the nature of Christ. How were the humanity and divinity of Christ to be safeguarded without the diminution of either? If, as orthodox faith insisted, Jesus was a single person in whom subsisted two natures, the one human and the other divine, then it would seem to follow that Mary was the mother of the person Jesus (one could hardly be the mother of a nature) and, as a consequence, bore God within her womb prior to the birth of Jesus. That was exactly what the Council of Ephesus defined in A.D. 431 when it legitimized the term *Theotokos* ("God bearer") as an apt title for Mary. "Thus, there is no doubt," said Saint Cyril of Alexandria's letter to the council, "that the Holy Virgin can be called *Theotokos.*"

While the "hidden" Mary of the ascetics continued to be honored in the church throughout the ages, the *Theotokos* doctrine gave great impetus to a treatment of Mary in a more solemn and exalted manner. After the fifth cen-

---

* Benedicta Ward, trans., *The Sayings of the Desert Fathers* (Kalamazoo, Mich.: Cistercian Publications, 1975), p. 157.

tury, largely in response to this appellation, the figure of Mary began to take on a sense of majesty and regality. We see that most clearly in the development of marian art. Both in the Byzantine East and in the Latin West, Mary was most often portrayed as seated on a formal throne or standing with the child presented to the viewer in a full frontal view. This kind of art is to be found in mosaics and icons as well as fresco and panel painting. Even the great madonnas done by Cimabue, Duccio, and Giotto on the eve of the Renaissance show this regality in a fashion that has roots in the patristic period.

Mary as *Theotokos*—or *Mother of God,* as she was called in the West after the time of Saint Ambrose (340–397)—was a constant theme in the mariology and the marian art of the early Middle Ages. Sometime in the twelfth century, theologians began to speak of Mary as crowned the queen of heaven. Some scholars place this idea's origin within the circle of Abbot Suger (1081–1151), who is famous for, among other things, being the founder of the Gothic style of architecture. That Suger presided over the royal abbey of Saint Denis, served for a period as regent of France, and acted as counselor to the French monarchy makes him (or his circle) a plausible source for concepts that present Mary in terms of coronation and queenship. At any event, the regality of Mary and the Gothic cathedral of the twelfth century are inextricably intertwined.

It may be well to pause and consider the relationship of Mary to the Gothic cathedral. The French town of Chartres is a good place to focus. For centuries, Chartres claimed to possess an important relic of the Virgin: her tunic. When this relic survived a disastrous fire that destroyed much of the cathedral in 1194, the people of the town accepted this as a sign that Mary favored their city. As a result, they raised the money and provided the manpower needed to build a new cathedral on the ashes of the old. The result of that outburst of civic enthusiasm is the present cathedral at Chartres, resplendent in its soaring architecture, sculpture, and incomparable stained glass.

The cathedral at Chartres, like the other great shrines of the Middle Ages, was not merely a mute monument symbolizing medieval devotion. it was, for the town, an important civic symbol and the crucial magnet for its economic prosperity. Pilgrims came from all over Europe to visit the cathedral and to honor the relics retained there. These crowds swelled on the four great feasts of the Virgin in the church calendar, when trade fairs were held to coincide with the religious solemnities: the Purification of Mary on February 2, the Annunciation on March 25, the Assumption of the Virgin on August 15, and the Nativity of the Virgin on September 8. It would not be entirely cynical to think that the many great windows in Chartres donated by the local guilds of craftspeople and merchants reflected both the medieval love of the Virgin and the timeless hope of profit. In short, the cathedral at Chartres stands as a complex monument to civic pride, popular devotion, an intricately worked-out theological iconography, and an economic base for the people.

The medieval love for the Virgin was not limited to the more palpable realities of great cathedrals. It was a genuine and widespread sentiment that gripped every class and condition in the medieval period. While it is not entirely possible to explain how this devotion rose to such intensity, most surely it developed through the compression of a number of cultural factors: the religiosity of the age in general, the ideals of chivalry, and the influence of the ideas of courtly love. The twelfth and thirteenth centuries were the marian period *par excellence.* That period produced the great cathedrals dedicated to her name, the intense marian theology of such writers as Saint Bernard of Clairvaux (1090–1153), popular devotions like "Mary's Psalter" (which eventually evolved into the rosary), and the great cycle of miracle stories involving the Virgin.

The highest expression of this intense marian piety may been seen in the poetry of Dante Alighieri. In the *Commedia,* Dante passes through hell and purgatory as part of a purificatory process to prepare him for the vision of God, which is at the apex of his visit to paradise. For Dante, the beatific vision was the culmination of life and the perfect fulfillment of the human intellect. In the final canto (xxxiii) of the *Paradiso,* Dante is ready for the vision of God. Beatrice, the symbol of divine grace, takes him to Saint Bernard of Clairvaux, who then intercedes before the Virgin (a significant fact in its own right: Mary mediates for those who wish to approach God) with a long prayer. That prayer, which comprises the first forty lines of the final canto (xxxiii) of the *Paradiso,* can be seen as a short summary of the highest aspirations of medieval mariology:

> Virgin Mother, daughter of thy son, lowly yet exalted more than any other creature, fixed goal of the eternal counsel,
> Thou art she who did so ennoble human nature that its own Maker did not scorn to become its making.

In your womb flamed again the love under whose warmth in the eternal
  peace this flower has thus unfolded.*
Here you are the meridian torch of love and there below with living
  mortals are a living spring of hope.
Lady, you are so great and have such worth, that if anyone who seeks out
  grace and flies not to thee, his longing is like flight without wings.
Your kindliness not only fills those who ask but often anticipates the
  request.
In you is tenderness, in you is pity, in you is liberality.
In you all that is created stands in high excellence.
Now he [Dante] who from the deepest part of the universe even to this
  height has seen the spirits living in their place implores you, by a grace,
  for enough power to lift his eyes higher towards the eternal bliss.
And I, who never burned for my own vision more than
I burn for his, proffer all my prayers and pray they may be enough
that thou disperse from him every cloud of mortality with your prayers so
  that the joy supreme may be opened to him.
Further do I pray, Queen most powerful, that you watch over him when the
  vision is over:
Let your protection smother human turmoil.
Look now on Beatrice who with many saints joins her hands in my prayer.

This prayer crystallizes in words the intense devotion to the Virgin that
was characteristic of Dante and of the times in which he lived. Earlier in the
Paradiso, Dante said that he invoked the name of the Virgin in prayer every
morning and every evening of his life (*Par.* xxiii — 88). In the *Purgatorio,* the
penitent souls, as they mounted the terraces representing the seven capital
sins, were purged as they meditated on incidents from the Virgin's life. In his
native Florence, Dante would have heard the *lauda* sung in her favor in the
Franciscan and Dominican churches. He most likely knew at first hand the
new approaches of marian art being fostered by artists like Giotto, whom he
mentions by name in the *Commedia.* Furthermore, it was in Dante's time that
the ancient Florentine cathedral, dedicated originally to Santa Reparata, was
being rebuilt under its new name: Saint Mary of the Flowers. Dante quite
possibly knew the story that Saint Bernard once had a vision of Mary in which
he received, from her breast, three drops of her milk as nourishment for his
own devotion to her.

---

* This line refers to the ''Mystic Rose'' of heaven where the saints dwell before God.

Saint Bernard of Clairvaux's prayer is, of course, "high" theology. Its cadences reflect the educated sentiments of Dante, who was both a highly literate person and a man of exquisite poetic sensibility. He was capable of the common touch, but in his poetry—especially in those final cantos—he strained for the majestic and the solemn.

For most of the populace of the medieval period, the sentiments of piety were hardly as lofty but every bit as passionate. Inspired both by the earthiness of the early Franciscan vision and the zeal of the Dominicans (who were indefatigable apostles of Mary), popular sentiment came to view the queen of heaven as the highly approachable "madonna." This madonna was, simultaneously, an inexhaustible conduit of sacred power and the mother of humanity in its deepest and most sentiment-ridden sense. A great deal of medieval piety emphasized, not the theses of schoolmen, but the instinctive truths of Mary's generous maternity. We need only compare the ethereal and hieratic Virgins of Italo-Byzantine art with the mature frescos of Giotto to see the difference. Gone (or increasingly more rare) are the golden backgrounds and the distant visions of the *Theotokos*. Instead, we find human and palpable figures of the Virgin: a real woman who has just given birth, or a real mother, struck dumb with grief, standing near her dead son, who has been horribly executed. Culminating this humanizing movement in late medieval art are those innumerable *Madonna with Child* works produced during the Renaissance. In those paintings, for all their virtuosity and splendor, the human femininity of Mary and the loveableness of an idealized infant come into prominence. The highest expression of that tendency can be found in the marian painting of artists like Fra Angelico (in whose works the medieval echoes are still present but muted) in the fifteenth century and Raphael in the early sixteenth century.

Most modern believers, one suspects, think of Mary either as a model to be emulated or as the saint, among all saints, to be honored. In an earlier time—and especially in the pre-modern period—the Virgin was seen as the great intercessor (who could soften the harsh demands of divine justice or approach the unapproachable divinity, an idea prominent in Dante) and, more importantly, the worker of miracles on behalf of her devoted clients. This last fact needs special emphasis if we are to comprehend the piety of medieval Catholicism. The Virgin could "break through" our mundane world to heal, warm, succor, strengthen, undo evil, and provide hope and sustenance for the future.

The great marian shrines and pilgrimage sites were focused centers of this manifestation of power. Even the great Roman basilica of Saint Mary Major, rebuilt to honor the *Theotokos* doctrine of the Council of Ephesus in the fifth century, is connected with legend. Pope Liberius, the story goes, built the original church on the Esquiline Hill in the fourth century because of a snowfall there in the month of August, which covered the exact site for the building and was interpreted as a sign from Mary herself. By the Middle Ages, imposing marian sanctuaries, sites of her miraculous intervention, multiplied in Europe as the medieval love for pilgrimage (and miracle) increased. Among the more celebrated pilgrimage goals associated with the Virgin founded in the Middle Ages include: Einsiedeln in Switzerland (ninth century), Our Lady of Walsingham in England (eleventh century), Mariazell in Austria (twelfth century), Our Lady of the Pillar in Saragossa, Spain (thirteenth century), Our Lady of Czestochowa in Poland (fourteenth century), and the House of the Virgin at Loreto in Italy (fourteenth century).

One other source of marian power was the relic. Relics were seen as links confirming the "realness" of the great figures of religion and as sources for spiritual power. Relics had been a central feature of Christian piety from the patristic age. In the Middle Ages, relics of the Blessed Virgin began to proliferate. One scholarly survey of medieval marian relics mentions over seventy locations where small amounts of the Virgin's breast milk were conserved, including one church in Naples that had the milk in liquid form! In the twelfth century, the Sicilian town of Piazza proudly claimed to own hairs from the Virgin's head; these relics then found their way to Messina, where a letter was also venerated, one supposedly written by the Virgin to the people of the city. We have already noted that Chartres had the tunic of Mary, and other places in France held other pieces of the clothing. At Sens, for example, there was a fragment of her dress, while a Paris monastery, beginning in the fifteenth century, claimed to have a sleeve from her dress. In Italy, the small Tuscan town of Prato venerated the girdle to the Virgin's dress, while the cathedral at Perugia claimed to possess the engagement ring of Joseph and Mary.

The educated class reacted intensely against this kind of credulous piety towards the close of the Middle Ages. Catholic reformers, like Erasmus, deplored the increasingly externalized religion of pilgrimage, relic, and shrine as passionately as they preached internal conversion and the emulation of saintly virtue. "Many Christians will light a candle to the Blessed Virgin, even at noon when it is unnecessary," Erasmus wrote in *The Praise of Folly*. "But how few have the ardent desire to imitate her in her chaste life, her temperance, and her love for spiritual things! For ultimately this is true worship and most pleasing to heaven." In the Protestant Reformation, despite a lingering marian devotionalism in the writings of Martin Luther, veneration of the Blessed Virgin was swept away with the same vigor and finality as monastic institutions, a celibate clergy, the Latin mass, and devotion to the other saints. For the Reformation, devotion to Mary derogated from the true worship of God in Christ.

The Catholic counter-reformation did legislate against the more obvious exaggerations of marian devotion but never wavered as to its basic legitimacy or its place in Catholic devotional life. The Council of Trent (1545 – 64) took pains to reffirm the legitimacy of relics and the spiritual use of artistic representations of the Blessed Virgin and the other saints. This reaffirmation was directed, of course, right at the rejection of the reformers. Reaction brings its own kind of reaction. As if to use marian devotion as a test of Catholic orthodoxy, the church during the seventeenth and eighteenth centuries, especially in Catholic countries, saw renewed interest in, and encouragement of, marian devotionalism. One measure of that fervor was the large number of feasts of Mary added to the Roman liturgical calendar during this period: the Feast of the Holy Name of Mary (1683), the Feast of Our Lady of Mercy (1690), the Feast of Our Lady of the Holy Rosary (1716), the Feast of Our Lady of Mount Carmel (1726), and the Feast of the Seven Sorrows of Our Lady (1727).

In this same counter-reformation period, there was an increase in the number of sodalities, religious confraternities as well as new religious orders of men and women devoted to Mary. The most extravagant of these were the groups who described themselves as "slaves of Mary." This rather baroque form of popular piety found its most eloquent spokesman in Saint Louis Grignion de Montfort (1673 – 1716) who wrote treatises on devotion to the Blessed Mother. The exuberant sentiment of his writing was matched only by that of the writings of his near contemporary, Saint Alphonsus Liguori (1696 – 1787), whose *Glories of Mary* went through numerous editions and remained popular well into this century. It is a mark of the appeal of this kind of lavish piety that the writings of Saint Louis de Montfort provided spiritual underpinnings for one of this century's most successful Catholic lay activist movements, the Legion of Mary, founded after World War I in Dublin, Ireland.

Parallel to these ecclesiastical developments were certain manifestations of marian piety in the world of culture. Although after the seventeenth century marian themes in art began to show symptoms of jejune sentimentality (there are clear signs of it in the art of the Spaniard Murillo, who was the greatest marian painter of his time), there was a vigorous musical tradition in the baroque era. A veritable explosion of masses, oratorios, and settings for marian texts was produced in the eighteenth century. One thinks immediately of the marian oratorios of Domenico Scarlatti (died 1757), the monumental setting for the "Magnificat" composed by Johann Sebastian Bach (died 1750), as well as the numerous settings for the *Stabat Mater* done by musical masters such as Vivaldi (died 1741), Haydn (died 1809), and Pergolesi (died 1736).

One would have thought that the French Revolution, the rising scientific spirit, the Industrial Revolution, and the winds of change sweeping over Europe would have muted popular manifestations of marian piety in the nineteenth-century church. Such was not the case. In fact, the nineteenth century saw in Roman Catholicism an explosion of devotion to the Virgin that almost rivalled the marian era of the Middle Ages. Scholars have noted that the embattled church saw in a renewed marian spirituality a way of stepping back from the battering forces of modernity. Unlike during the Middle Ages, however, when this surge of devotion seems to have sprung up from the grass roots, the marian piety of the last century was fostered and promulgated by the leadership of the Catholic church. The first great moment in this renewed marian era was, of course, the definition of the dogma of the Immaculate Conception by Pope Pius IX in 1854. We might, for symmetry's sake, close the era a century later with the Marian Year of 1954, proclaimed by Pope Pius XII, the same pontiff who had defined the dogma of the Assumption of the Blessed Virgin into Heaven on August 15, 1950.

These great papal events mark off a century. In that same period, almost in open defiance of a disbelieving world, the church accepted as credible a series of apparitions of the Blessed Virgin. Revelations to Catherine Labouré (canonized in 1947) in Paris between 1830 and 1836 gave rise to the pious custom of the "miraculous medal" dedicated to the Immaculate Conception. This event, according to many scholars, gave Pope Pius IX the impetus to define the doctrine of the Immaculate Conception less than twenty years later. Apparitions to a French peasant girl named Bernadette Soubirous in the Pyrennes town of Lourdes in 1858 began what was to develop into the greatest and largest marian shrine center of our time. Anyone who has ever visited Lourdes—with its unbelievably vulgar pious souvenir shops outside the sanctuary (and its equally vulgar architecture within!), its legions of sick who come to bathe in its healing waters, its candlelit processions in the evening, its constant sounds of the Lourdes hymn, and its cavelike grotto where, it is said, the Virgin appeared to Bernadette—can get some contemporary feel for what a pilgrimage site of the Middle Ages must have been like. A similar pilgrimage site at Fatima in Portugal marks the place where the Virgin appeared to three young shepherd children in 1917. Lesser known shrines that also celebrate modern apparitions would include Knock in Ireland and Beauraing in Belgium.

Again, as in the post-Tridentine period, modern pontiffs reinforced these manifestations of marian piety by the institution of new liturgical feasts in honor of Mary for the universal church. In 1904, for example, Pope Saint Pius X established a feast day to commemorate the apparitions of Our Lady at Lourdes, which gave liturgical approval to the visions of Bernadette Soubirous, herself later canonized as a saint. In 1931, Pope Pius XI named October 11 as the Feast of the Divine Maternity of Mary. Pope Pius XII made October 31 the Feast of the Immaculate Heart of Mary, and in the Marian Year of 1954, he designated May 31 as the day the church would celebrate the Queenship of Mary. To these liturgical titles, Pope Paul VI added "Mary, Mother of the Church" during the days of the Second Vatican Council.

A good deal of both the more exuberant forms of marian devotion and much of advanced mariological speculation (for example, Mary as Mediatrix of Grace, Mary as Co-Redemptrix, etc.) was based on the notion of *De Maria numquam satis.* But was it true that there could never be enough said about the Virgin? Certainly, one could plausibly argue that many forms of devotionalism were a question of style, taste, and cultural temperament. Was there not much justice and forthrightness in Cardinal Newman's personal observation in the *Apologia Pro Vita Sua* apropos of some forms of continental devotional practices: "Such devotional manifestations in honor of our Lady had been my great *crux* as regards Catholicism; I say frankly, I do not enter fully into them now; I trust I do not love her the less, because I cannot enter into them. They may be fully explained and defended; but sentiment and taste do not run with logic; they are suitable for Italy, they are not suitable for England."

At the sessions of the Second Vatican Council, the issue was less the taste of devotionalism and more the place of mariological speculation in the framework of theology itself. Many of the conciliar Fathers wished to see a separate document devoted to mariology. This move was resisted by those who felt that mariological speculation had developed too discretely. In the end, after real divisions of opinion, the conciliar statement on Mary was made part of the *Constitution on the Church*. Its inclusion in that document was a conscious effort to link mariology more closely to the more central foci of theology. Pope Paul VI, in fact, told the assembly of the council that it was "the first time an ecumenical council presented such a vast synthesis of the place of Mary in the mystery of Christ and the church."

The work of the Second Vatican Council was not an attempt to "downgrade" the Blessed Virgin Mary (as even some of the bishops there thought). Instead, it was an attempt to understand Mary, not as a discrete entity, but in relation to the entire Christian mystery. In its exhortation to theologians, one senses the balance that the conciliar Fathers wished to see reflected in church devotion to the Virgin:

> It exhorts theologians and preachers of the divine word to abstain zealously both from all gross exaggerations as well as petty narrowmindedness in considering the singular dignity of the Mother of God. . . . Let them assiduously keep away from whatever, either by word or deed, could lead separated brethren or any other into error regarding the true doctrine of the church. Let the faithful remember moreover that true devotion consists neither in sterile or transitory affection, nor in a certain vain credulity, but proceeds from true faith by which we are led to know the excellence of the Mother of God, and we are moved to a filial love towards our mother and to the imitation of her virtues. (*Constitution on the Church* VIII, iv, 67)

For all the balance and nuance recommended in the conciliar statements, there was a noticeable decline of popular marian piety in postconciliar Catholicism. Only a decade after the council, Garry Wills would look back with genuine nostalgia on "May processions in the warm night air of Summer. . . . Scapulars like big postage stamps glued here and there on kids in swimming pools . . . the fifty-nine beads and assorted medallions of the rosary . . . the sight in darkened churches of a shadowy Virgin with hands held palms out at the level of her hips, plaster cape flowing down from those hands towards blue votive lights unsteady under her like troubled water."*

Though the simple marian piety of bygone ages seems in decline, it is far from dead. Devotion to the Virgin, if more scripturally and theologically rigorous, is still part of the Catholic tradition. Its more popular forms can show up in startling ways. While North American visitors have been traditionally scandalized by the intense devotionalism of the Mexican peasants who walk across the plaza of the shrine of Our Lady of Guadalupe, it must be doubly bewildering for the Anglo-Saxon to see formerly mute *braceros* organize in the agricultural areas of the American Southwest under the banner of that same Virgin. The *braceros* of today know their tradition. Their forebears did the same thing in the revolutionary days of Zapata at the beginning of the century.

And it must be equally a matter of chagrin for the Marxist theoreticians to explain the magnetlike attraction of the shrine of Our Lady of Czestochowa in Poland. However, it is less puzzling when one remembers the roots of this shrine in the national consciousness of Poles. The figure of the Virgin, after all, still bears the saber scar of a much earlier unbeliever. In neither case does the devotion of Mary equal that peasant fatalism often ascribed to such popular piety. In fact, the Virgin has often been the energizing symbol of social aspiration. Both the Virgin of Guadalupe and the Virgin of Czestochowa manifest the traditional role of the Virgin: a mother who is a protector. What one should remember in this regard is that a mother can be fiercely—even dangerously—protective of her children. It may be one of the small ironies of religious history that as devotion begins to wane in those "Christian" countries that first nourished it, her appeal is showing forth in the seething Third World or in the suppressed culture of Eastern Europe. Ironic, yes—but not all that surprising, since the figure of the *Theotokos* has been one of the more resilient symbols in the history of religion.

---

* Garry Wills, *Bare Ruined Choirs: Doubt, Prophecy and Radical Religion* (Garden City, N.Y.: Doubleday, 1972), pp. 35–36.

Major Shrines and Sanctuaries

of the Blessed Virgin

Argentina   Our Lady of Luján

Belgium   The Shrine of Our Lady of Beauraing

Bolivia   Our Lady of Copacabana

England   Our Lady of Mount Carmel (Aylesford)
     The Shrine of Our Lady of Walsingham

France   The Shrine of Our Lady of LaSalette
     The Shrine of Our Lady of Lourdes
     Our Lady of the Miraculous Medal (Paris)
     Notre Dame Cathedral (Paris)
     Our Lady of Chartres

Greece   The "Holy Mountain of Our Lady" (Mount Athos)

Israel   The Basilica of the Annunciation (Nazareth)
     The Church of the Visitation (Ain Karim)
     The Basilica of the Nativity (Bethlehem)
     The Church of the Dormition (Mt. Zion)

Italy   The Basilica of Saint Mary Major (Rome)
     Our Lady of Perpetual Help (Church of San Alfonso, Rome)
     The Madonna of Saint Luke (Bologna)
     The Holy House of Loreto
     The Shrine of Our Lady of Tears (Syracuse)

Mexico   The Shrine of Our Lady of Guadalupe

Poland   Our Lady of Czestochowa
     Our Lady of Koden

Portugal   The Shrine of Our Lady of Fatima

Spain	The Black Madonna of Montserrat
	Our Lady of the Pillar (Saragossa)
Switzerland	The Black Virgin of Einsiedeln
Turkey	The House of the Virgin (Ephesus)
U.S.	The National Shrine of the Immaculate Conception
	Our Lady of the Conquest, "La Conquistadora" (Santa Fe, New Mexico)
	Our Lady of the Milk (Saint Augustine, Florida)

For Further Reading

There is a goldmine of marian lore in the many entries on Mary in the *New Catholic Encyclopedia* (New York: McGraw-Hill, 1967). Although the biblical discussion is outdated, there is an immense body of later marian material in the entry "Maria" of the *Biblioteca Sanctorum* VII (Rome: Lateran, 1967). Juniper Carol's three-volume *Mariology* (Milwaukee: Bruce, 1964) is dated, but still serviceable. Of the many theologians who have written on Mary, Karl Rahner has produced a work that seems both sensible and profound: *Mary, Mother of the Lord* (New York: Herder and Herder, 1963). Geoffrey Ashe's *The Virgin* (London: Routledge and Kegan Paul, 1976) argues for an independent marian church in the patristic period. Eamon Carroll's "Theology of the Virgin Mary," *Theological Studies* (June, 1976), pp. 253 – 89, exhaustively surveys the marian literature for the decade after the council, while providing fine leads for future bibliographies. John A. Saliba's fascinating "Virgin Birth and Anthropology," *Theological Studies* (September, 1975), pp. 428 – 54, provides a glimpse of current debates over Mary as symbol in recent anthropological literature. For a splendid essay on the dense signification of a marian symbol in terms of its social role, one can profitably read Eric Wolf's "The Virgin of Guadalupe: A Mexican National Symbol," in *Reader of Comparative Religion*, edited by Lessa and Vogt (New York: Harper & Row, 1972), pp. 226 – 30.

Mary and Contemporary Experience

One does not have to be a doomsayer to understand that the religious experience of these waning years of this century is quite different from that of past ages. Looking at the great marian art of the past can trigger emotions of nostalgia and even puzzlement. There is great faith today, but it is faith that comes at a price. We are no longer close to the turning of the seasons, the world of nature. We fight to keep our sense of religious mystery in a world that emphasizes, not mystery, but problems. We are no longer permitted the luxury of naivete. To recover the religious simplicity of a Giotto or the ineffably sweet faith of a Fra Angelico seems beyond our ken.

That such a piety is behind us may be a matter of sadness, but it should not be a reason for despair. Every age has its sense of lost innocence and ours is no exception. When we try to puzzle out the significance of a religious tradition like that of Mary, we are faced with the serious obstacles set up by our own location in time; we are not, as a cultural majority, located close to the world of nature or free from the abstractions of urban life. Our theology is pulling away from the past that once shaped it. The background of classical civilization and the metaphysical worldview of the medieval period are not part of us. We carry their influences because we are a traditional people. Traditions, however, are steps on the way.

Every age must look back on its traditions not as an antiquarian who wants to collect, but as an architect who wants to build. To discuss the place of Mary in contemporary experience, then, we must look back at the past while keeping an eye on the present. That this is happening in the contemporary church seems patent. The very pressures of ecumenical discussion (and criticism) has triggered an immense re-evaluation of almost every area of Christian concern. Since the marian tradition has been such an identifying mark of the Catholic tradition, it is understandable that it also has received attention in our age—both to understand its historical meaning and to assess its contemporary significance.

It has been a commonplace of anti-Catholic polemics to compare marian devotionalism to the pagan cults of antiquity. Worship of Mary, this argument would insist, is nothing more than a reflection of the syncretistic impulses of Catholicism by which the forgotten (or not-so-forgotten) goddesses of antiquity become translated into a new, and lightly Christianized, version of the pagan queen of heaven or the *Magna Mater* of Mediterranean fertility religion. After all, pagan antiquity abounded in virginal mothers; for every painting or statue of the Virgin and Child in a Christian church, one could find pagan analogues in the antiquity museums of the world. True Christianity, this argument concludes, centers on God in Christ alone, with no diminishment of *his* centrality. More specifically, these critics would argue, popular marian devotion smacks too much of the old religions over which Christianity triumphed. Furthermore, there is too great a correlation between Mary and celibate chastity, a value that is overappreciated in the Catholic tradition.

As one browses through the history of marian devotionalism, there seems to be some truth in these observations. The innumerable figures of Mary nursing her child, the statues that, in the estimation of the faithful, represent the hope of barren women, the curative shrines with their caves and healing springs—all of these have the aura of a past that is not only pre-Christian but prehistoric. Mary, in the popular imagination, either continued the maternal and fertile powers of the ancient goddesses or supplanted them. It is not merely an accident of geography that the shrine of Our Lady of Guadalupe was built over the ruins of the pre-Hispanic shrine to *Tonantzin*, the Aztec goddess mother whose symbol, like that of the Virgin, was the moon. Missionary friars, a hundred years after the Virgin's shrine was built (it was completed in the late sixteenth century), still complained that it was "the purpose of the wicked to worship the goddess and not the Holy Virgin, or both together. . . ." What the missionaries did in Mexico replicated what had been done elsewhere and earlier. At times, the very name of the church indicates the triumph of the Virgin over pagan antiquity. In Rome, for example, there is a fine Gothic church called *Santa Maria sopra Minerva*—Saint Mary over (the shrine of) Minerva.

Catholics are not insensitive to these charges. Whatever the excesses of folk Catholicism, the church argues, Mary is always affirmed as creature, not deity. She is, as Dante wrote, *figlia del figlio suo*—daughter of her son. Even those maximalist theologians who wished to extend the doctrinal formulations on Mary to include such terms as "Mediatrix of all Grace" or "Co-Redemptrix" were quite careful to phrase those possibly misleading titles in a very circumscribed way. The participants at the Second Vatican Council, as we have already noted, were alert to non-Catholic (the "separated brethren" of the documents) reactions to mariological formulations. There seems little doubt that the final decision not to issue a separate conciliar document on Mary (something passionately desired by the maximalists) was motivated both to rein in the more exuberant formulations of mariology and to reintegrate mariological formulations into a larger (and more ecumenical) theological framework. As one English Benedictine abbot said at the time, the decision not to have a distinct document on Mary was made because such a document could provide no check on marian maximalists' "more extravagant flights."

The formal work of the Second Vatican Council ended in the mid-1960s. That was precisely the period when feminism first began to articulate its theoretical manifestos and organize itself as a coherent public movement. Betty Friedan published her landmark *The Feminine Mystique* in 1963; three years later, she was instrumental in founding the National Organization for Women (N.O.W.). The rapid rise of feminist activity in the decade that followed had its influence in the churches where women (and men) began to investigate the place and role of women in the church from the perspective of the feminist critique of sexism in general. This investigation was all the more urgent because feminists indicted the churches as bastions of anti-feminine sentiments.

In any such discussion it was inevitable that the role of Mary in the formation of attitudes about women in the Christian tradition should receive particular attention. Not surprisingly, there was less than complete unanimity on the significance of Mary when the matter was subjected to a feminist critique. At first, these intramural debates, fierce as they were, were confined to a highly intellectual class of theologians and cultural critics. The debate, however, became heated enough for the Vatican to be aware of it. In an exhortation on the Blessed Virgin, delivered in 1974, Pope Paul VI acknowledged these debates, yet he insisted that Mary could serve as a model for modern women if they could understand that the forms and tastes of the past are not necessarily normative. "It should be considered quite normal for succeeding generations of Christians in differing socio-cultural contexts to have expressed their sentiments about the mother of Jesus in a way and a manner that reflected their own age," the pontiff observed.

There, as a subtext, is the crux of the matter. In what "way and manner" can the Virgin speak to our age and our world?

In the rather overpraised *Alone of All Her Sex: The Myth and Cult of the Virgin Mary* (1976), British writer Marina Warner says that, for modern women, the Virgin has been emptied of moral significance. Mary has lost her force and, with it, the power either to heal or to harm. Warner argues that Mary, as the figure of a woman who is a mother but has not experienced either sexuality (Mary ever Virgin) or the pangs of childbirth (Virgin *in partu*) is set "alone of all her sex" beyond feminine experience. Such a "setting apart" invites invidious comparison with the rest of women and, as a consequence, denigrates them. This paradox reflects a deeper dichotomy in Catholic teaching between its teaching about the sacramental goodness of the natural world and its deep strain of pessimistic asceticism, which, in its world denial, overpraises virginity at the expense of bodiliness. For feminist critics like Warner, the Virgin reflects a kind of profound schizophrenia in Christianity. Mary is honored as the ideal feminine but, in that very act of honor, other women are degraded. Such a bifurcated attitude is simply one other reflection of that tendency to idealize women or put them on a pedestal in order to hold in check their inherent femininity and sexuality. However rich the past tradition that honored Mary might be, it is based on premises no longer palatable for modern consciousness. Hence, Warner's apodictic judgment: Mary's day is over.

Christian feminists, fully aware of the misogynistic elements that accompany much of traditional mariology, could not fully accept that severe analysis. Those theologians wish to re-examine the traditions of mariology in the context of the patriarchal and masculine bias of the Christian tradition. Can the significance of Mary be seen without reference to that tradition? What,

from a feminist perspective, is one to make of—just to cite one example—
the popular tendency to see Mary mediating the desires of humanity before
an implacably stern and just God? Elizabeth Schussler-Fiorenza's observations help us to see how a feminist perspective might recover value from a
traditional notion:

> All the New Testament images and attributes which characterize God as
> loving, life giving, compassionate, and caring, as being with the people of
> God are now transferred to the "Mother of God," who is as accessible as
> was the nonpatriarchal God whom Jesus preached. Even though any Catho-
> lic school child can explain on an *intellectual theological* level the differ-
> ence between the worship of God and Christ and the veneration of Mary,
> on an *emotional, imaginative, experiential* level the Catholic child experi-
> ences the love of God in the figure of a woman. Since in later piety Jesus
> Christ became so transcendentalized and divinized that his incarnation and
> humanity are almost totally absorbed into his divinity, the "human face" of
> God is almost solely experienced in the image of a woman. The cult of
> Mary thus grew in proportion to the gradual repatriarchalization of the
> Christian God and Jesus Christ. The Catholic tradition gives us thus the
> opportunity to *experience* the divine reality in the person of a woman.*

The strong dichotomy between the severe Christ and the mediating
madonna may be poor theology but it is a persistent theme in marian devotion. It is persistently present in Christian art from the Middle Ages on and
ubiquitous in popular art. I once possessed a holy card depicting Mary
"fishing" souls into heaven with a rosary while Saint Peter, unaware of her
activity, implacably guarded the main gate to paradise. One extreme example
of this tension between the compassionate mother and her stern son may be
seen in a message that Mary gave to the young visionaries at LaSalette in the
last century: "Since my people are not willing to submit, I am forced to let go
my Son's hand. It is so heavy, so weighty, that I can no longer restrain it."

The ability to experience God through feminine imagery, about which
Professor Schussler-Fiorenza spoke, also provided a rich feminine language
about the divine in general. The cult of Mary manifested emotive possibilities
for the articulation of religious sentiment through the agency of feminine
language. Is this language important? The late Paul Tillich thought that any

---

* Elizabeth Schussler-Fiorenza, "Feminist Spirituality, Christian Identity, and Catholic Vision," in
Womanspirit Rising, edited by Plaskow and Christ (San Francisco: Harper & Row, 1979),
pp. 138—39.

god language that used male (or, for that matter, female) language exclusively was gravely impoverished. According to Tillich (in his *Systematic Theology*), male symbolism triumphed in the Reformation. The rather feminine Christ of pietism, Tillich argued, stood to a stern masculine God the father in a relation similar to Christ and Mary in Catholicism. The vigorous marian language and symbolism of the Catholic counter-reform accounted, in part, for its noticeable success against the Reform (marian devotionalism was, as we have already noted, a key ingredient of Tridentine and baroque Catholic piety). It further served, for those who hungered after such language, as a powerful magnet to draw many from the Reform to both the Roman and Greek church.

Tillich did not believe that the Reformed tradition could reinstate the Virgin as a symbolic power. That should not prevent an attempt at sexual balance in its theology. God, the "Ground of Being" seen as symbolic of the "mother quality of giving birth, carrying, and embracing, and, at the same time, of calling back, independence of the created, and swallowing" could help right an impoverished masculine bias. Tillich's point seems not unlike that of Carl Jung, who saw in the 1950 definition of the Assumption of the Virgin by Pope Pius XII an historical and long overdue reintegration of the polarities of Western consciousness between masculine and feminine, earth and heaven, and spirit and body.

A search for theological insights in the marian tradition would have to proceed in a manner that would loosen Mary from the oppressive ties that bind. Rosemary Ruether sees that Mary as:

> . . . the reconciled wholeness of women and men, nature and humans, creation and God in the new heaven and the new earth. In her, God already shows mercy and might: the proud are scattered in the imagination of their hearts; the mighty are put down from their thrones, while the humiliated are lifted up; the rich are sent away empty, and the hungry are filled with good things. With such a Mary women might even be able to say "My soul magnifies the Lord and my spirit rejoices in God my saviour." (Luke 1:46—47)*

The possibilities of this reconceptualizing of mariological categories are numerous. Attention could be given, to cite a few more prominent examples, to the tradition of the *mulier fortis*. There is a long tradition, both theological

---

* Rosemary Radford Ruether, "Mistress of Heaven: The Meaning of Mariology," in *New Woman, New Earth: Sexist Ideologies and Human Liberation* (New York: Seabury, 1975), p. 59.

and liturgical, of linking this "valiant woman" of the *Book of Proverbs* with the figure of Mary. Such links occur mainly with respect to "power" titles of the Virgin. They serve as a healthy antidote to the self-effacing Mary seen in so many marian traditions. The "valiant woman" takes on a greater aura of dignity and regality when these usages are further linked to the image in the *Book of Revelation* of the woman who is surrounded with the celestial signs of the stars, sun, and moon.

Another—and much understudied—theme is that of Mary as priest. It would be most instructive to go back over the history of that usage in the light of the current debate over women's ordination. What, for example, is one to make over this curiosity: in the first decades of this century, the church approved for use prayers to the Virgin that describe Mary as a priest (Pope Pius IX in the last century actually used the term in official correspondence) while, during the same period, the Holy Office (in a decree promulgated in 1916) forbade the use of any image of the Virgin that had her dressed in priestly garments. Themes of this sort could be multiplied from the marian tradition; they cry out for sustained inquiry.

To approach mariology in this manner is not to force it to fit the procrustean bed of feminist ideology. It is, rather, to deepen those insights that the tradition, because of cultural pressures, has chosen to ignore or underplay. It is, further, as much an exercise in theology as in mariology. As Andrew Greeley has noted, a deeper appreciation of what he calls rather inelegantly the "Mary Myth" is to seek to understand, not Mary, but how God is revealed in Mary and through marian language.

Greeley's point deserves emphasis, if only because it ties together a number of themes raised by feminist theologians. A study of the marian tradition does not only permit us to see how Mary functioned in the Christian tradition. It also gives us precious clues as to how to deal with deep theological language using the feminine idiom. There has been a concerted effort over the past decade to think of traditional theological categories and their relationship to masculine language and ideology. To what degree can we recover the deep sense of God without dependence on the patriarchal categories and images inherited from the past? Must we simply scrap that past and start afresh as radical thinkers like Mary Daly suggest? Or, are there alternative sources available to us? It is the argument of more than one contemporary writer that the tradition of mariology, freed from its more culturally offensive formulations, could provide a starting point for a feminine language of transcendence.

Insights of this kind, hard won by theologians who must struggle with inherited intellectual systems, come connatural to many of those who approach Mary with what I would call the mentality of "shrine" religion. These devotees of her popular cult (let the marian shrine stand as a sort of shorthand for this entire phenomenon of popular devotion to Mary) provide much insight into the nature of her true significance even though that significance is hard to articulate at a conceptual level.

It is commonplace criticism to say that the marian shrine can mask ideological sentiments. We have seen that happen in our own time in an aberrant sort of way. In the past decade, a series of apparitions alleged to have occurred in Bayside, New York, illustrate how Mary can be marshaled as a witness to current religious turmoil. The Virgin told her devotees there that the real popes, since Vatican II, have been imprisoned and that the voices of the Vatican which preach ecumenism and condemn the Catholic Traditionalist Movement are the voices of the anti-Christ who act as agents of Satan. Such revelations put a heavenly seal of approval on the labors of the followers of Archbishop Marcel Lefebvre and his integralist followers. It is not the first time that the Virgin has been put to the service of reaction.

Ideology is not the only thing that one sees when considering marian shrines. The anthropologists note the caves, the grottos, the *ex voto* offerings, the "sacred precincts," and see in those shrines manifestations of some of the earliest impulses and appurtenances of preliterate religion. The socially minded skeptic will see peasant credulity and clerical manipulation—Mary as the opiate of the masses. Fastidious believers will see vulgarity—a religion of the *Lumpenproletariat* unworthy of the purer flights of spiritual or theological rectitude. Those unsympathetic to the Catholic tradition will see ill-digested paganism, relics of syncretism, malfunctions and distortions of biblical religion.

But, if one affirms the genuine religious sentiment in this piety—which most surely exists—then we can rightly ask about its shape and significance. Can one step aside from, or suspend judgment about, the specific cultural cast of this or that shrine in an attempt to see beneath to the essence of the thing? There is one generalization that we can offer. The pilgrims who go to Lourdes, Fatima, Loreto, or Guadalupe do all say this one thing: the world is graceful—gracefilled. Whether they petition for health, express their faith in times of political or cultural crisis, or ask the Virgin for protection against the vicissitudes of nature or history, they all implicitly affirm that *things do not have to be this way*. The world, and our place in it, can be made more coherent, just as pain and bewilderment can be assuaged. The cosmos is not indifferent nor is it opaque. There is, of course, little empirical evidence for this attitude, which is precisely why it is called faith.

That such aspirations and affirmations are brought before a woman specifies the character of this trust. Marian faith affirms a belief in the transcendental quality of maternal concern, protectiveness, compassion, power, and intervention. The revolutionary potential in such a faith finds itself in the implicit motif that "things do not have to be this way." Popular religion may preach stasis, but it can also preach change—change of the person or his social state. The banners of Our Lady of Guadalupe, which guided Zapata in 1910 and the striking *braceros* of the 1970s, signalled that the Mother did not wish her children to live the way they did. One of the reasons why the church has been cautiously skeptical about alleged apparitions is because it recognized that beneath the mask of credulous piety can lurk powerful, even revolutionary, aspirations for alternatives. The faith manifested in popular piety, however extravagant its cultural manifestation, is as old as religious aspiration itself.

This popular piety seems now to be gaining the interest of those theologians who wish to understand the dynamics of the religion of the poor. Liberation theologians note the binding power of this religion and its potential for deepening the consciousness of its devotees. They wish to thread their way through those formulations that alienate and oppress to find the powerful symbols of life and freedom. Such potentiality is there. Charles Peguy was right in his observation that all religion begins in mysticism and ends in politics. In marian devotion one notes the continuation of the oldest impulses of religious expression acted out in the turbulent fields of history. It is that combination which is so heady with promise.

Marian piety blends together the oldest urges of nature religion with the cultural traditions of the Bible. It speaks of fertility as well as of redemption. It is close to the world but yearns to encompass it. It is, as Gerard Manley Hopkins once concluded in his lovely poem "The Blessed Virgin Compared to the Air We Breathe," an *atmosphere*:

Be thou, then, O thou dear
Mother; my atmosphere;
My happier world, wherein
To wend and meet no sin;
Above me, round me lie
Fronting my forward eye
With sweet and scarless sky;
Stir in my ears, speak there
Of God's love, O live air,
Of patience, penance, prayer:
Worldmothering air, air wild,
Wound with thee, in thee is led,
Fold home, fast hold thy child.

Hopkins' poem reflects a faith in the reality of Mary as a truth that is cosmic in its scope. Mary becomes more than a person; she is a real part of the world in which the believer moves. The very world of nature is an antiphonal hymn testifying to the reality of the Virgin beyond doctrines and devotion. While the sentiments are pure Hopkins, the truths that undergird them are ancient and honorable. No one can look at marian devotion without catching the echoes of nature, seasons, doctrine, and devotion. Hopkins' poem is simply a compressed version of the traditional marian devotions celebrated in May—"Mary's Month"—with its panoply of flowers, garlands, young girls, and the Queen Mother honored in the promises of the late Spring. The sentimentality of the occasion cannot overcome the sincerity and depth of the poetry expressed in the May hymn: "Oh, Mary, we crown thee with blossoms today/Queen of the angels/Queen of the May."

Can this kind of piety breathe the air of modernity and still live? Does the precipitous decline in traditional marian piety in the developed West simply presage what will happen when that same air begins to circulate over Mexico and Haiti and the other less-developed lands? Will intense marian devotion survive in any Marxist state in which the winds of liberal democracy blow? Is it resistance (rather than piety) that stiffens the will to be a child of the madonna? Marian piety, for a large part of the developed world, seems now more an exercise in nostalgia than a vital or dynamic source of inspiration. It does not seem accidental that those newspapers and journals most antipathetic to the changes of Vatican II also seem the most fervent supporters of traditional marian piety. One can hardly walk through the mock

Byzantine national shrine of the Immaculate Conception in Washington, D. C., without feeling that one is strolling through a vast monument to a now dead past.

These are difficult questions and hard sayings. One must not be premature. The "death of Mary" may be as precipitous a prophecy as was the demise of God announced with such finality by Nietzsche in the last century. There is deep wisdom in Santayana's quip that "there is no God and Mary is his mother" since the foundations of marian devotion were laid long before the patriarchal gods. Mircea Eliade has observed that basic religious symbols do not die, nor do their basic structures change; they simply acquire new meanings under the pressure of history and throughout the course of time.

It may well be that the rise of feminism coincidental with the last manifestations of triumphal mariology was providential. If Mary is the "new woman," as the ancient Christian tradition affirms, then her place in the larger theological and devotional life of the future church will take a radical turn, a turn that will yield new insights into the seamless web of Christian belief. To discover those insights will require both a sense of the salvageable past and a radical openness to the possibilities of the future. It will require that we resist both the temptation to see the past as frozen in timeless amber and the temptation to reject the past as unworthy of the present or irrelevant to the future. Christian revelation is mediated through language and sign, but that revelation is, at bottom, mystery. Our grasp of it is limited both by the finitude of language and by our own existential finitude. It is for that reason that, as believers, we are always on pilgrimage to the not-yet-present.

The marian tradition, so amply illustrated in the art and photography of these pages, is rich and ancient. It represents the mind, the heart, and the genius of our past culture. As it unfolds, it demonstrates both continuity and innovation. It speaks of basic human attitudes intertwined with abstruse theological speculations and fundamental motifs of human folklore. It is a *sacramentum* of the collective faith of millenia. It is a rich lode to be mined, since it contains hints of how we are to live and clues about how we may believe. Marian devotion is both a history of our faith and a pointer to our future.

For Further Reading

On the larger issue of women in the Catholic theological tradition, George H.

Tavard's *Woman in Christian Tradition* (South Bend, Ind.: University of Notre Dame Press, 1973) is rich with insight. For a sociological approach to the marian shrines, Alan Neame's *The Happening at Lourdes: The Sociology of the Grotto* (New York: Simon and Schuster, 1967) is that rarest of phenomena in social science: a book that is both learned and readable. On the place of marian theology and social reaction, William McSweeney's *Roman Catholicism: The Search for Relevance* (New York: St. Martin's Press, 1980) is most helpful. Andrew Greeley's *The Mary Myth: On the Femininity of God* (New York: Seabury, 1977) is typically Greeleyesque: pugnaciously irritating and unfailingly insightful. Heiko Oberman's *The Virgin Mary in Evangelical Perspective* (Philadelphia: Fortress, 1971) gives a Protestant perspective, as does the much older work by G. Miegge, *The Virgin Mary: The Roman Catholic Doctrine* (Philadelphia: Westminster, 1953). For feminist perspectives, besides the material cited in the text, I have found useful Rosemary Ruether, ed., *Religion and Sexism: Images of Woman in the Jewish and Christian Tradition* (New York: Simon and Schuster, 1974), as well as her brief *Mary: The Feminine Face of the Church* (Philadelphia: Westminster, 1977). There are some interesting, if superficial, observations on mariology and liberation theology in Harvey Cox's *The Seduction of the Spirit* (New York: Simon and Schuster, 1973).

116

Marian Prayers and Devotions

Sub Tuum Praesidium
(From the late third century)

We fly to thy patronage, O Holy Mother of God. Despise not our petitions in our necessities; deliver us always from all dangers, O glorious and blessed Virgin.

Memorare

Remember, O most gracious Virgin Mary, that never was it known that anyone who fled to thy protection, implored thy help, or sought thy intercession was left unaided. Inspired with this confidence, I fly unto thee, O Virgin of Virgins, my Mother. To thee I come; before thee I stand, sinful and sorrowful. O Mother of the Word Incarnate, despise not my petitions, but in thy clemency hear and answer me.
Amen.

Salve Regina

Hail! Holy Queen, Mother of Mercy, our life, our sweetness, and our hope! To thee do we cry, poor banished children of Eve; to thee do we send up our sighs, mourning and weeping in this valley of tears! Turn, then, most gracious Advocate, thine eyes of mercy upon us, and after this, our exile, show unto us the blessed fruit of thy womb, Jesus. O clement! O loving! O sweet Virgin Mary.

A Hymn of Praise to Mary
(From the Byzantine Liturgy)

It is proper to call you blessed, ever-esteemed Theotokos, most pure, and mother of God. You who are more worthy of honor than the cherubim and far more glorious than the seraphim. You who incorruptibly gave birth to God the Word, verily Theotokos, we fervently extoll you.

Antiphons of the Blessed Virgin

I

(Alma Redemptoris Mater)

Loving mother of the Redeemer, open door to heaven and star of the sea, come quickly to the aid of your people, fallen indeed but determined to stand again. To nature's astonishment you were the mother of your holy Creator without ceasing to be a Virgin, and heard from greeting "Hail!" Have pity on us sinners.

II

(Ave Regina caelorum)

Hail, Queen of heaven; hail, Mistress of the angels; hail, root of Jesse; hail, the gate through which the Light rose over the earth.

Rejoice, Virgin most renowned and of unsurpassed beauty.

III

(Regina coeli, laetare)

Queen of heaven, rejoice, alleluia. The Son whom it was your privilege to bear, alleluia, has risen as He said, alleluia. Pray God for us, alleluia.

A Prayer to Mary
(Attributed to Thomas à Kempis)

Hail, Mary, full of grace, the Lord is with thee. Hail, hope of the needy, Mother of those who no longer possess a mother. O Mary, when my broken heart moans and is filled with sorrow, when my soul is enveloped in sadness and fear, when the wind of temptation blows, when stormy passions break loose in my soul, when my sins have closed the gates of heaven against me and robbed me of the friendship of my God, in this hour of tribulation and anguish, to whom should I have recourse but to thee, O Blessed Mary, consoler of the afflicted and refuge of sinners?

O Mary, thou art indeed that beautiful star of the sea, who saves all those who in the hour of danger raise their eyes to you. I cry to you, then, for help this day, O most merciful Mother of God! I fly to thee with the confidence with which little children take refuge in their mother's arms. Open thine to me: give me the right to take shelter in thy heart; let me hear from your lips the sweet words: "Fear nothing. I am your advocate, I will plead for you: as a mother consoles her weeping child, I will console you." My Mother, say these words, and peace will return to my heart. Come, O Mary, come, with thy constant sweetness, to visit me in my sorrow. Come to raise my courage, to bring me the grace of Jesus. May thy name, full of grace, be, with the adored name of Jesus, the last name I pronounce on earth.

Amen.

Selected Praises of Mary from the *Agathistos* Hymn
(Greek—sixth century)

Hail, thou, the restoration of the fallen Adam; hail, thou, the redemption of the tears of Eve.

Hail, height, hard to climb, for human minds; Hail, depth, hard to explore, even for the eyes of angels.

Hail, thou that art the throne of the King; hail, thou who sustains the sustainer of all.

Hail, thou bride unwedded.

Hail, thou initiate of the ineffable counsel; hail, surety of those who beseech thee in silence.

Hail, heavenly ladder by which God came down; Hail, bridge leading from earth to heaven.

Hail, thou who gave birth to the Light; Hail, thou who withheld the divine secret from all.

Hail, thou bride unwedded.

Hail, branch of unfading growth; hail, wealth of unmingled fruit.

Hail, thou who revives the green fields of joy; hail, thou who prepares a haven for souls.

Hail, favour of God to mortals; hail, access of mortals to God.

Hail, thou bride unwedded.

Hail, Mother of the Lamb and of the shepherd; hail, fold for the sheep of his pasture.

Hail, bulwark from invisible foes; hail, opener of the gates of paradise.

Hail, never silent voice of the apostles; hail, never conquered courage of the champions.

Hail, thou bride unwedded.

Hail, mother of the star that never sets; hail, dawn of the mystic day.

Hail, thou who cast out the inhuman tyrant of old; hail, thou who show forth the Lord, the merciful Christ.

Hail, guide of the wisdom of the faithful; hail, joy of all generations.

Hail, thou bride unwedded.

Hail, uplifting of men; hail, downfall of demons.

Hail, sustenance in succession to manna; hail, messenger of holy joy.

Hail, land of promise; hail, thou from whom flows forth milk and honey.

Hail, thou bride unwedded.

Hail, Flower of incorruption; hail, crown of chastity.

Hail, space for the uncontained God; hail, door of solemn mystery.

Hail, vessel of the wisdom of Good; hail, treasury of his foreknowledge.

Hail, thou bride unwedded.

I Sing of a Maiden
(Anonymous English medieval poem)

I sing of a maiden
That is makeless:*
King of all kinges
To her son she ches.*
He came all so stille
There his mother was
As dew in Aprille
That falleth on the grass.
He came all so stille
To his mother's bower

As dew in Aprille
That falleth on the flower.
He came all so stille
There his mother lay
As dew in Aprille
that falleth on the spray.
Mother and maiden
Was never none but she;
Well may such a lady
Goddes mother be.

*makeless: matchless
*ches: chose

In Praise of Mary
(Anonymous medieval poem in English)

Of one that is so fair and bright,
  velut maris stella
Brighter than the day's light,
  parens et puella
I cry to thee; thou see to me!
Lady, pray thy Son for me,
  tam pia
that I might come to thee,
  Maria.

Lady, flower of all things,
  Rosa sine spina
Thou bore Jesu, heaven's king
  Gratia divina.
Of all thou bear'st the prize
Lady, queen of paradise
  Electa.
Maid mild mother is
  Effecta.

Of caring counsel thou art best
  Felix fecundata,
For all weary, thou art rest,
  Mater honorata.
Beseech Him with mild mood
That for us all hath shed his blood
  In cruce,
That we might come to Him
  In Luce.

All this world was forlorn
  Eva peccatrice,
Till our Lord was born
  De te genetrice.
With "Ave" it went away
Darkest night and cometh the day
  Salutis.
The well springs out of thee
  Virtutis.

Well he knows he is thy son
  Ventre quem portasti;
he will not deny thee thy boon,
  Parvum quem lactasti.
So kind and good he is,
He has brought us to bliss
  Superni,
That hath shut up the foul pit
  Inferni.

The Titles of Mary from *The Litany of Loreto*

Holy Mary

Holy Mother of God

Holy Virgin of virgins

Mother of Christ

Mother of Divine Grace

Mother most pure

Mother most chaste

Mother inviolate

Mother undefiled

Mother most amiable

Mother most admirable

Mother of good counsel

Mother of our Creator

Mother of our Saviour

Virgin most prudent

Virgin most venerable

Virgin most renowned

Virgin most powerful

Virgin most merciful

Virgin most faithful

Mirror of Justice

Seat of Wisdom

Cause of Our Joy

Spiritual vessel

Vessel of Honor

Singular Vessel of Devotion

Mystical Rose

Tower of David

Tower of Ivory

House of Gold

Ark of the Covenant

Gate of Heaven

Morning Star

Health of the Sick

Refuge of Sinners

Comfort of the Afflicted

Help of Christians

Queen of Angels

Queen of Patriarchs

Queen of the Prophets

Queen of Apostles

Queen of Martyrs

Queen of Confessors

Queen of Virgins

Queen of all Saints

Queen conceived without original sin

Queen of the most Holy Rosary

Queen of Peace.

The Mysteries of the Rosary

JOYFUL MYSTERIES
The Annunciation
The Visitation
The Nativity of the Lord
The Presentation of Jesus in the Temple
The Finding of the Child Jesus in the Temple

SORROWFUL MYSTERIES
The Agony in the Garden
The Scourging at the Pillar
The Crowning with Thorns
The Carrying of the Cross
The Crucifixion and Death of Our Lord

THE GLORIOUS MYSTERIES
The Resurrection
The Ascension of Christ into Heaven
The Descent of the Holy Spirit upon the Apostles
The Assumption of the Blessed Virgin into Heaven
The Coronation of the Blessed Virgin Mary in Heaven.

The Seven Sorrows of the Blessed Virgin

1) Mary presents her Child in the temple, and Simeon the prophet predicts that her heart will be pierced with a sword.
2) Mary flees with Saint Joseph and the Infant Jesus to escape the murderous wrath of King Herod.
3) Mary loses her Son when visiting the temple in Jerusalem.
4) Mary sees her Son bruised and crushed under the weight of the Cross as he goes to Calvary.
5) Mary stands at the foot of the Cross as her son suffers and dies.
6) The body of the lifeless Christ is put into her arms at Calvary.
7) She follows the body of her Son as it is put into the tomb and the sepulchre is sealed.

Feasts of the Blessed Virgin Mary in the Roman Rite

January 1: Solemnity of Mary, the Mother of God

February 2: The Purification of Mary/ The Presentation of the Child Jesus in the Temple (Candlemas Day)

February 11: Our Lady of Lourdes

March 25: The Annunciation

May 31: The Visitation

May (variable): The Immaculate Heart of Mary

July 16: Our Lady of Mount Carmel

July 26: Sts. Joachim and Anna, the parents of Mary

August 5: Dedication of the Basilica of Saint Mary Major (Our Lady of the Snows)

August 15: The Assumption of the Blessed Virgin Mary into Heaven

August 22: The Queenship of Mary

September 8: The Birth of Mary

September 15: Our Lady of Sorrows

October 7: Our Lady of the Rosary

November 21: Presentation of Mary in the Temple

December 8: The Immaculate Conception

Color Plate Captions

Jacket
Our Lady of Czestochowa, Poland.

Page 1
Holy water font depicting madonna and child; marble and glazed polychrome terracotta; vestry of Santa Maria Novella, Florence, Italy; Giovanni della Robbia, 1498.

2−3
Little Sisters of Mary, a new religious order at Colle Pino, near Assisi, Italy.

4−5
Flight of steps leading to the Church of Our Lady of Remedios; azulejos (traditional Portuguese tile work) depicting the Coronation of the Virgin; Lamego, Portugal.

6
Detail from flight of steps from above church depicting the Annunciation and the Marriage of Mary to Joseph.

7
As above, depicting Madonna with Child and the Assumption.

8
The Visitation of Mary to Elizabeth; from the Book of Hours; Meermano Museum, Den Haag, Holland (painted 1515−1520). Simon Bening (Flemish).

17
Our Lady of Koden, altar in basilica at Koden, Poland; statue of saint holding portrait of Our Lady of Czestochowa.

18
Volunteer lay helpers of the Unitalsi organization, who help the faithful to the Sanctuary of Loreto, Italy.

19
Pilgrims at sanctuary of Our Lady of Caacupe, Paraguay.

20
Our Lady of Consolation; fresco in Santa Maria Maggiore, Assisi, Italy; fourteenth century.

21
Our Lady of Wisdom; St. Peter's Cathedral, Louvain, Belgium.

22−23
Annual procession in Koden, Poland.

24
The Holy Family at table; fresco, Sanctuary of Miedniewice, Poland; sixteenth century.

37
The birth of Mary; Carrara Museum, Bergamo, Italy; Vittore Carpaccio (Venetian, 1450−1522).

38
St. Anne and Mary; El Prado Museum, Madrid, Spain; B. E. Murillo (Spanish, 1617−1682?).

39
Presentation at the Temple; Museum of the Academy, Venice, Italy; Titian (Venetian, 1490−1576?).

40−41
The Annunciation; St. Mark's Convent, Florence, Italy (painted ca. 1430); Beato Angelico (Florentine, 1400−1455).

42
The Visitation; Pieve di Santo Stefano, Carmignano, Florence, Italy; Jacopo Pontormo (1494−1556).

43
Marriage of the Virgin; Brera Museum, Milan, Italy (painted for the Franciscans at Città di Castello); Raphael Sanzio (1483−1520).

44
Expectant Virgin; Monterchi, Italy; Piero della Francesca (1420−1492).

45
Daily life in Nazareth; azuelejo, Church of Our Lady of Remedios, Lamego, Portugal.

46−47
Nativity; Church of Santa Chiara, Assisi, Italy; painter unknown; fourteenth century.

48–49
The Adoration of the Magi; National Gallery, Washington, D. C. (painted ca. 1482); Sandro Botticelli (Florentine, 1444–1510?).

50
Virgin with Child; Catacomb of Commodilla, Rome, Italy; sixth century.

Mother of God (Theotokos); Hagia Sophia, Istanbul, Turkey.

Virgin and Child; Book of Kells, 760–820.

Madonna with Child; Seminary of Saint Francis, Siena, Italy; A. Lorenzetti (1280?–1348).

Virgin and Child; Peter Paul Rubens (1577–1640).

Virgin and Child; Haitian primitive painting.

51
Renaissance altar with Byzantine icon; Church of S.S. Benedetto and Scolastica, Venice, Italy.

52
Purification; from *Les tres riches heures du Duc de Berry*; Musée Condé, Chantilly, France; early fifteenth century.

53
Flight into Egypt; Uffizi Gallery, Florence, Italy; Gentile da Fabriano (1370–1427?).

54
Christ among the doctors; Academy, Florence, Italy; Taddeo Gaddi (Florentine, 1300–1366?).

55
Marriage at Cana; fresco from the Scrovegni Chapel, Padua, Italy; Giotto (Florentine, 1266?–1337).

56
The Crucifixion; Mary and St. John at the foot of the Cross; San Sepolcro, Italy; Piero della Francesca (1420–1494).

57
St. John consoling the Virgin; Convent of Christ Church, Tomar, Portugal; polychrome statue attributed to Munoz.

58
Pieta (detail); Museum of Brera, Milan, Italy; Giovanni Bellini (Venetian, 1430?–1516).

59
Death of the Virgin; El Prado Museum, Madrid, Spain; A. Mantegna (Paduan school, 1431?–1506).

60
The Assumption; Church of Santa Maria Gloriosa dei Frari, Venice, Italy; Titian (1490–1576).

77
Our Lady of the Rosary; on hilltop outside Coimbra, Portugal; twentieth century.

78
Little Sisters of Mary, dressed for religious observances; Colle Pino, Italy.

79
As above, dressed for work.

80
Statue of Our Lady of Fatima, carried in procession, Portugal.

81
Statue of Our Lady of the Snow, carried in procession, Portugal.

82
Votive offerings from Our Lady of Remedios, Cholula, Mexico.

Votive plaques from Sanctuary of Our Lady of the Miraculous Medal, Paris, France.

Reliquary in Sanctuary of Zapopan, Guadalajara, Mexico.

83
Madonna with votive offerings; St. Catherine's Church, Viano de Castelo, Portugal.

84–85
Indian pilgrims in procession in front of the Sanctuary of Guadalupe, with Our Lady of Guadalupe portrayed on the flag; Mexico City.

86
Madonna with boat, Protectress of Sailors; Viano do Castelo, Portugal.

87
Girl dressed as the Virgin in a Portuguese pageant.

88 – 89
Angel, Mary, St. Anne, and child; polychrome wood altar piece; Benedictine Monastery, Pombeiro, Portugal.

90
Our Lady of Remedios, Protectress of the Spanish troops in the Mexican War of Independence (at the same time that Our Lady of Guadalupe was the Protectress of the Insurgents); chapel in Cholula, Mexico.

91
Women carrying flowers on the steps of the above chapel.

92
Madonna with child and fourteenth-century model madonna; Cathedral Treasury, Viseu, Portugal.

105
Madonna of the Sanctuary of Loreto during a night procession on the feast of the Immaculate Conception, Italy, 1981.

106
Man praying at the Sanctuary of Beauraing, Belgium, 1981.

107
Lay helpers receiving communion at the Sanctuary of Loreto, Italy, 1981.

108
Pilgrims at Lourdes, France.

109
Nuns carrying holy water at Lourdes.

110
American singer Retta Hughes, as Mary, performing in "Black Nativity" for Pope John Paul II; Rome, Christmas, 1981; costume by Myrna Colley-Lee.

111
Sister Lupina of the Order of the Assumption teaching Indians in Mexico, 1982.

112
Chapel in the Monastery of Christ in the Desert, Abiquiu, New Mexico, 1982.

113
Our Lady of Walsingham; Sanctuary of Walsingham, England.

Chapel of the Assumption, Walsingham, England.

114
The courtyard of one of the houses where the Holy Family supposedly rested on the flight into Egypt; Cairo, Egypt.

115
Entrance to the former Church of the Virgin; Ephesus, Turkey.

116
A field of flowers near Ephesus.

117
Roadside shrine to the Virgin in Greece.

118 – 119
The House of the Virgin, the home where Mary is believed to have settled after Jesus' death; Ephesus, Turkey.

120
Our Lady of Guadalupe, Spain.